Contents

KU-506-936

Being a
Film Producer

Kathy Galashan

Published in association with The Basic Skills Agency

Hodder & Stoughton

A MEMBER OF THE HODDER HEADLINE GROUP

Acknowledgements

Cover: Corbis

Photos: p 2 Jean Cummings/All Action; pp 5, 25 Moviestore Collection/© Disney Enterprises, Inc.; p 9 Stefan Rousseau/Topham Picturepoint; p 12 Clive Barda/PAL; p 18 Moviestore Collection; p 20 © James P Blair/Corbis

Every effort has been made to trace copyright holders of material reproduced in this book. Any rights not acknowledged will be acknowledged in subsequent printings if notice is given to the publisher.

Orders; please contact Bookpoint Ltd, 39 Milton Park, Abingdon, Oxon OX14 4TD. Telephone: (44) 01235 400414, Fax: (44) 01235 400454. Lines are open from 9.00–6.00, Monday to Saturday, with a 24 hour message answering service.
Email address: orders@bookpoint.co.uk

British Library Cataloguing in Publication Data
A catalogue record for this title is available from the British Library

ISBN 0 340 77523 8

First published 2000
Impression number   10 9 8 7 6 5 4 3 2 1
Year   2005 2004 2003 2002 2001 2000

Copyright © 2000 Kathy Galashan

Typeset by GreenGate Publishing Services, Tonbridge, Kent.
Printed in Great Britain for Hodder and Stoughton Educational, a division of Hodder Headline Plc, 338 Euston Road, London NW1 3BH, by Redwood Books, Trowbridge, Wilts

1 Being a Film Producer

I'm Susan.
I live in Los Angeles.
I'm a film producer.

I want to make a million dollar film.
It's a thriller.
I've got a great idea
but I haven't got a million dollars.

I'm going to make a four minute trailer.
The trailer will give an idea of the film.
Then I can ask people
and studios for money.

Do you want to know
what a film producer does?

I'll tell you about a week
in my working life.

This is the week we make the trailer.
I'm working with the Director.
The Director's job
is to turn the script into a film.
He tells the actors and camera people
what to do.

A film producer

2 Monday

The trailer will be filmed in one day.
Friday is the day for filming.
I have a meeting
with the script writer.
We check the script
and make a few changes.

There is a phone call from an agent.
My lead actress has got chicken pox!
I need a new actress.
I make some phone calls.
I have to set up auditions.
I call two other agents.

I check the locations for Friday.
The locations are the places
the filming takes place.
We need a street scene and a cafe.

Today I'm taking the Director
to the locations.
We drive out and find the room.
It's big and empty.
We can bring in things
to make it look like a café.
It's good.

I check the electrics
and parking space.
There are going to be
15 people in all.
There is space
for people to get dressed
and space for people to eat.

I get a call from an agent.
She has four actresses
to audition tomorrow.

I call the lead actor.
Can he come in
and help at the audition?

Working on location with the cast of *The Three Musketeers*.
© Disney Enterprises, Inc.

I call Wardrobe,
the person in charge of clothes.
I tell her we will have
a new actress.

I call to check that
cameras have been rented.

Money is a problem.
Five people promised money.
The trailer will cost $10,000.
I have spent $2,000 of my own money.
It's all gone.
I need $8,000 more.
I'm spending as little as possible.

I phone the lawyer
to check contracts are signed.
They are not ready yet!

3 Tuesday

The Director and I
meet lighting and camera people.

I get a call from the writer.
I've got to pay him $500
if I use the script for the audition.
I promise him $250 today and $250 on Friday.

We set up a room for the auditions.
My lead actor turns up.
He says he can't film on Friday.
He's got tickets
for a big football game!
I spend half an hour talking to him.
I can't change the day of the shoot.
He understands.

The first actress comes.
She's too thin and looks wrong.
The second actress can't act.
The third actress is great
but too expensive.

The fourth actress is good
but she has never been
in a film before.
She may not be free on Friday.
She will call tomorrow.

Auditioning for actors and actresses.

I call another agent.
I may need more auditions tomorrow.

The Wardrobe Assistant calls.
She needs to buy a dress
for the new actress.
I ask her to wait.

The lawyer calls.
The contracts are not ready.
The people with the money
are worried about the lead actress.
So am I!

4 Wednesday

We go back to the location.
We can rent the room for two days.
I have to pay $400.

We have to find lots of things.
The room has to look like a cafe.
We need tables, chairs
and wine bottles.
We need blinds for the windows
The floor is too light.
We have to paint it.

The actress calls back.
It's fine, she'll do it.
We can now buy clothes.

I have a meeting
with Wardrobe and Make-Up.

A member of the cast being made up.

I set up a rehearsal
at my house for 6pm.
We can't use the room yet.

The Writer calls.
He wants to change the script.
He has a great idea for a new ending.

I have a meeting
with the Director and the Writer.
We can try out the new ending at rehearsal.

I call the Caterer
who is doing the food.
He will do breakfast, lunch and dinner.
Good food keeps everybody happy
and is very important.

The lawyer calls.
I can have the money
tomorrow at 1pm.

We have a rehearsal.
The new ending is great.
The actor and actress
are very good together.

There's a problem.
The actress has dark hair.
We need someone with blonde hair.
I talk to the actress.
She agrees to colour it.
Make-Up agrees but it's an extra $50.

5 Thursday

Tomorrow is the big day.
I make lots of calls.
I need people for small parts.
I call friends to help out.
I check everyone knows
how to get to the location.
We are starting at 5am.

Wardrobe fits clothes.
The actress looks good with blonde hair.

I call the lawyer.
No answer.

I make sure the cameras, film
and equipment is ready.
I listen to some tapes.
The film is going to need music.

The lawyer calls.
The money is OK.
GREAT!

I check the location.
Is the café set up?
It isn't.
The paint on the floor is wet.
We can't put anything down until 6pm.

In the evening we get the café ready.
We finish at midnight.

6 Friday

5am. People arrive.
The lead actor and actress
get dressed and made up.

A camera lens is missing.
I call up the camera place.
A friend picks up the missing part.

We have breakfast.

The room looks good.
The lighting looks good.
We have a quick rehearsal.

We start filming.
The actors are good.

I'm getting nervous.
The Director is taking too much time.
We won't finish filming today.
I make him go quicker.

Filming

Lunch.

We move onto the street
and film outside.
Aeroplanes keep going past.
We have to do it 10 or 11 times.

It's 11pm.
The shoot is over
and people go home.
I drive the film to the lab.
They develop the film overnight.

Checking camera angles

7 Saturday

The Director and I check the film.
One street scene is a little dark.
We decide we can't do it again.

The week is over.
We are really tired.
Filming is finished.

8 After the Shoot

After the shoot, editing starts.
The film has to be put together.
The Director and I work with the Editor.

We look at all the film
and choose the best bits.
Then we add music, titles and credits.

The trailer is finished
but now I have to raise $1,000,000

I set up meetings with film studios
and backers.
If they think the film will make money,
they will back it.
If I can get famous actors interested,
they will back it.

If I get the backers,
I can make the film.
If the film is a success,
I'll make a lot of money.
There are a lot of 'ifs'!

9 A Good Producer

What is a good producer?

He or she has good ideas.
She is creative.
She can get a good team of people together.
She can solve problems.
She can raise money.

It's hard to make a film or TV programme.
A good producer makes it look easy.

Running through the scene with members of the cast of *George of the Jungle*. © Disney Enterprises, Inc.

10 How to Become a Producer

There isn't one way.
Most producers work their way up.

They start as an assistant.
Just getting any job
in the business is the first step.
Often they don't get paid
for their first job.

Some people start with a video camera
and make short films on their own.
Some people go to film school.
Some people have family or friends
who help them.
Some people have money
and buy their way in.

People who make films
have one thing in common.
They eat, sleep and think films
24 hours a day.
Being a producer is a way of life,
not just a job.

Glossary of Terms Used

THE PEOPLE

Agent   Finds work for an actor.

Lead actor
Lead actress } The person in the main part.

Backer   Provides money for a film.
                   Sometimes called an investor.

Camera person Works the cameras.

Director   Turns the script into a film.
                   Tells actors what to do.

Editor   Puts the film from a shoot together.
                   Makes cuts and changes
                   so that the finished film looks good.

Lawyer   Deals with contracts and legal matters.

Lighting   Works the lights.

Make-Up   The person in charge of hair and
                   make-up.

Wardrobe	The person in charge of clothes.
Audition	An interview an actor goes through to see if they are right for the part.
Budget	The amount of money there is to spend.
Contract	An agreement that people stick to.
Location	The place where a film is set.
Shoot	Filming.